ENCOURAGEMENT

My Book of Psalms

CRISTA L. TARPLEY

Encouragement: My Book of Psalms
Copyright © 2022 Crista L. Tarpley

Because of the dynamic nature of the Internet, any web addresses or links contained in this book may have changed since publication and may no longer be valid. The views expressed in this work are solely those of the author and do not necessarily reflect the views of the publisher, and the publisher hereby disclaims any responsibility for them.

Library of Congress Control Number: 2023931416
Paperback: 978-1-960362-00-1
eBook: 978-1-960362-01-8

CONTENTS

Dedication

*Thanking God first, without him this book would not have happen.
To my huband, Dr. Jimmy L. Tarpley, to my children, April and
Solangelo, Janice my gaurdian child, and to their husbands: Tim,
Tony and their children, Timmie and Antonio, My sister Kerry,
Gertrude, Faye, and Maria. My brother Fred and wife Shirley.
Thanks to Shirley Terry who inspired me with encouraging words, to
the Mt. Olive Baptist Church family, the Chatham Middle School
family, thanks to all of you. To the publishing ocmpany, thank
you for making this possible. I truly hope when people read this
poetry book it will inspire them to not give up, but to strive on.*

IN MEMORY OF

This book is dedicated in the memory of my later father and mother, Hugh and Christabell Payne Wilson. To Etters and Classie Leftwich Tarpley my father and mother-in-law. To the later Oderal Haley my sister in Christ, to the late Pearl Younger my sister in Christ. To the late Lucille Tarpley Wilson, grandmother. To all of the family and friends that have gone on to be at rest. We love you but God loved you best

AGENDA

Rose to the morning sun, thanked Christ for another run.
Rose with a word of prayer, asks Christ for mercy everywhere.
Turned greedy family members, address letters to senders.
Put my war clothes on, to manage things if going wrong.
Watched for backbiting, stealing, and dwelled on love,
forgiveness, and healing.
Took one step at a time, watched how situations fell in line.
Never over plan your agenda and becomes a total hindrance.
Blessed agenda I must say, Christ was on board today.

A CHANGE WILL COME

Should I fall to the bottom or stand still and holler?

Should I pray, fast, or wait; or should I continue to hate?

Cannot go complain to friends, they want to know how long

and when. Our necks are tired in a rope, as if there is no hope.

Challenging task will be completed if prayed up and

not deleted.

Never let go of Gods' hand changes will come in his name.

Coming trials will be over, rejoice as a four- leaf clover.

Faith is our guide even with things we have not seen.

A GOOD CHILD

A good child will go bad when losing parents, they once had.
Cannot go any further when pressured by others.
When put down and constantly nagged,
this child will eventual turn bad.
Did not get the glory but complaints but stood tall and said I ain't.
Dismissed good trying to impress; went deeper and made a mess.
Put me down for the last time but will not ever whine.
Can we help this child to focus and not become a shell locust.

AM NOT

Am not an important thing but I am growing.

One who is establishing, accomplishing, and sowing.

Not one who can do everything but can-do certain things.

Will get over the hump, when not pushed to the front.

Not a person to be notice or praise, if it happens will be amazed.

Not one to put on a show then move out and lay low.

Not one to never offer a hand or help one in quicksand.

Not the one to misuse friends, will help to the end.

Will talk about a brand-new city, will not dwell on pity.

Not one to say it is the end, must run until I win.

BALLGAME

Team waiting to play when a voice yells delay.

A broken bridge waits ahead, please do not be misled.

Strike one there is trouble, strike two it is double.

Strike three total hardships, strike four situations flips.

Could not seem to climb back when the team went off track.

Team needs to start the game and do it in Gods' name.

This game introduced to all and can join or fall.

Mission we can complete if Christ comes to our defeat.

Christ gave us a chance to accept yet some will be left.

Watch, wait for the date, Christ will not be late.

BEEN AROUND

Been around awhile, walked many miles.
Beautiful Black intelligent wife, who took a view of her life.
Destruction took place on every side, no place I could hide.
Dislikes came in forms and caused serious harm.
Been around to see hatred increase, individuals
asking will there be a relief.
Storms forming in this land, people heating up their fans.
Been around, been around I must say, Christ will bring a new day.
Seek for new relationship and did find new fellowship.

BELIEVE

Believe that your injured heart will mend, and trials will end.
Believe that there will be no more tears, joy will not turn to fear.
Believe that hope will come your way and
happiness will shine each day.
Believe trouble will last for a while and bring a happy smile.
Things will be all right if we never remove Christ out of our life.

BEWARE

Beware of strangers you meet; beware of people washing your feet.
Be careful of people offering help; may take all with nothing left.
Beware when criticizing your fellowman;
may be the one to lend a hand.
Beware of how you mistreat others; may be your biological brother.
Beware of things you attempt to do; may come back to torment you.
Beware of close friendships; never let it attach your hip.
Beware of individuals knowing it all; it may become a down fall.
Beware of those not seeing trouble, it may come back double.
Beware of demanding conclusions it can produce a serious delusion.

BE STILL

Wanted to get mad, scream like dad.

CHRIST SAID BE STILL

Wanted to say you were wrong and do not mean harm.

CHRIST SAID BE STILL

Cannot take anymore when trouble knocked on my door.

CHRIST SAID BE STILL

Ran to seek cover, could not find shelter.

CHRIST SAID BE STILL

Went off on an adventure it was a true lecture.

CHRIST SAID BE STILL

Treated me like dirt thought I was a flirt.

CHRIST SAID BE STILL

Tried to do my best, saw me as less.

CHRIST SAID BE STILL

Tried to understand, doing the best I can.

CHRIST SAID BE STILL

Individuals walked over me, as if not seeing thee.

CHRIST SAID BE STILL

BLACK CHILD THIS IS FOR REAL

When are you going to learn that time is
passing, and people are clashing?
Doors closing in your face, as others are moving in fast pace.
Individuals needs a hand; turn and join a destructive band.
No mind in learning today; blaming others
for their unsuccessful ways.
Now knowing how to read, acting like an old bad seed.
Refusing to listen to father or mother, not listening to no others.
Never learned how rough life would be, never considered being free.
Die and never become great, while others have patience and wait.
Black brother's Black sister's tomorrow is not
promise, but today accomplish all you can.

BLESSING

Woke up this morning another blessing,
heart beating with no stressing.
Mind clear as can be after Gods' angels watched over me.
Got up moving, singing, and praying,
found out I was still in the land.
Continue to thank God for blessings today, as
I went along on my journey anyway.
Gave this day my best, returned home again to my nest.
Thank God once again for his grace and mercy in
this place and could see smiles on family's face.
Reminiscing over blessings gain; was sunshine and not rain.
Woke up again blessed; it was Gods' mercy and nothing less.

BONES

Light color brownish tone; nothing but a long bone.
Bones managed easy or light; forced with extreme might.
Bones huge others small, will break with a sudden fall.
God assembled all, put together by the holy one.
Dry bones no breath in sight, lying around with no movement or life.
Bones shaped the form of a body, Gods' creation and no hobby.
Bones ribs, legs, thighs, and back, skin covered the entire pack.
Breathed breath into this creation, was not any limitation.
Great rumbling came that day when bones
connected in a glorious way.
All at once bones began to move, knew that hope was coming soon.
Bones large medium and small; stood as an army and did not fall.
Bones made for tuff work, if moved wrong they will hurt.
Created a smile to bring warmness; created love with total gladness.
When life is over for these bones they will
return to dust and assemble home.

BUDDY

Buddy, strong big and white, guarded our home day and night.

Buddy, ran with strength of a lion, shook the ground as if in Zion.

Buddy, had a strange black tongue, cleaning it was no fun.

Acted like a child when in trouble, guess he
thought corrections would be double.

When bad dogs came around, Buddy
responded like a crazy bloodhound.

Going to the doctor he knew right away; joy ride was not that day.

Stopping by the doctor received a shot; Buddy was upset and hot.

Arrived home he was free, ran around chasing me.

Off to the creek to take a bath, came back with mud on his face.

He left one day did not return, family thought he was in harm.

Looked down the road saying any day, and no one had nothing to say.

He died or was picked up by a stranger, I pray
that Buddy was watched over by an anger.

CAN'T LOSE IT

Cannot lose your sight must remain tight.

Cannot lose your strive and take a deep dive.

Cannot lose the abilities and destroy the liberties.

Do not lose the faith and it turns into hate.

Cannot lose hope but learn how to cope.

Remain sober therefore will not be walked over.

Cannot lose your stand yes Christ is holding our hand.

Do not lose direction and turn into satisfaction.

CAN YOU REACH ME

Deep dark cold down here, body wrapped in total fear.
Want someone to grab me, evil tormenting thee, and can't see.
I cannot open the door here; evil is hanging everywhere.
Screamed for someone to pull me through;
evil tells me not to trust you.
Mind is not functioning right cruel to everyone in sight.
Lost in a body of evil a lost person and a deceiver.
Mind says focus on doing well, keep the soul from going to Hell.
Evil deep down in my soul trapped in a Big Black hole.
Know you are trying to reach me, do not know who it can be.
Tramped charitable deeds in the ground, mind silence with no sound.
Can anyone help me to escape, evil says no in his name's sake.
Can anyone reach me or am I late, do not want to miss the date.
Good mind cries out with tears bad mind says no big deal.
Trying to do my best, evil will not give me rest.
Can you reach me or am I too late, do not want to turn into hate.
Please try to reach me if you can, don't let me die insane.   15.

CAN YOU SEE IT

Laughter we once had is gone, talking too much on the gossip phone.
Love we shared has faded away, brought so many dull days.
Shared lots of beautiful dreams, now constantly setting off steam.
There is nothing we really have to say,
because anger stands in our way.
To have peace is it possible, or have communication and being stable?
Time is upon us to regain trust and for us to get rid of the fuss.
Whether we are right or wrong, can we just get along?

COMPLETE SILENCE

Silence is time to think, eyes focus no time to blink.

Silence is a moment of peace, OH! What a great relief.

Find a comfort Zone with no one speaking in a loud tone.

Silence is to empty the mind, while meditation deep upon time.

Nobody there to interrupt the quietness when

there are moments of sadness.

Forgetting about all the wrongs, dismissing all the harm.

Silence obtains thoughts in the mind, brings

beautiful memories oh! So, kind.

Gain strength through grace, put a happy smile upon the face.

Silence can be a completion after dealing with other durations.

COME HOME

Watching you I wanted to reach out, held my
peace and did not open my mouth.
Sadness was upon your face; your eyes twinkled in a glaze.
Wanted to cry out baby please come home,
did not want to use an angry tone.
Wondered what more can one take, before
the body crumble and break.
Concerned about what to say, you will come home one day.
Home is no longer the same when not touching your hand.
A mind to do right but evil took over your sight.
Can you please come back because loneliness is a fact?
One day will reach you and you will be home then.

COULD NOT HEAR ME

I needed courage, there was discourage.
You push me away, destroyed my day, and
never attempt to hear anyway.
Was in total distress did not know how to get out
of this mess, when attacking the flesh.
You did not feel the pain or see tears falling like rain.
Will anyone be there holding my hand and tell me I am not insane.
Eyes yelled help! Many walked away and left.
Closed the door, fall to the floor, then I gave it to God.
Christ is my true angel, ensured me of no danger.
Got up regain strength, now a strong link, stood tall did not sink.

CRY NOW REJOICE LATER

Cried early today when issues went another way.
No sun shining, people outrage whining, while others are lying.
Heartaches came with pain, thick drops of
rain, now tore out of the frame.
Became an adaptive learner, when striving like a soldier.
Heard Gods' voice, my heart rejoiced, got rid of the noise.
Answer came in time, after seeing the sign, now doing fine.
Cried now rejoice later because I have obtained a true savior.
Lord took my hand, helped me to understand,
now walking in Jesus' name.
Joy came on yesterday, brighten my day, and
trouble moved out of the way.

DARKNESS

Darkness destroys caring lose out on sharing.

Darkness lost in space with no signs of a familiar face.

Darkness no regain will create pain.

Darkness cast a shadow as if nothing really matters.

Darkness causes loneliness and destroys one's gladness.

Nobody will hear your call when darkness cause one to fall.

Darkness will end a life when putting up a fight.

However, Christ will change one's mind and will do it in time.

DEATH A BEAUTIFUL THING

Death does not say you need to get ready.

It does not move fast or in a hurry.

It is silent as a baby sleeping when over, individuals are weeping.

Death does not call certain people; anyone can stand tall and fall.

Pray that one soul is right death travel as a thief in the night.

Death chooses us one by one will come back for all and not some.

Scream and say I cannot go but we all will travel through the door.

Death will not say I will be back tomorrow;

it will knock and bring sorrow.

May not understand but death is coming to set the soul free.

Death will show up when not expected; claim children selected.

We should be ready when death comes,

rejoice, and go peacefully home.

DEVASTATED

I wanted to be free, but you stood around me.

Closed my eyes to regain self, felt like there was nothing left.

Body was in a rage and the heart was in a serious stage.

Walls began to cave in, started asking the Lord when.

Family members saw me as dead, but Christ was still the head.

Could not move or blink, so I settle down to think.

I really wanted water but could not even holler.

Tried seeking cover to protect self from all others.

Cannot give up now because I was going to come around.

Though of the devastation, Christ granted me

hope along with a new Revelation.

DIDN'T DESERVE IT

You hurt me but will smile, need me just dial.
Focused on right, caused a fight, it was tight.
Create to love, as a pure white dove, and to share hugs.
However, moved into another Zone, was
not alone, with a different tone.
Looked saw success, did not dwell on mess, Christ managed the test.
Thought I would be depressed but moved away
from stress and now graciousness.

DICTIONARY

Dictionary is my friend, started back when.

Dictionaries keeps the mind sane to travel in the right lane.

Words go from A-Z definitions of one, two, and three.

Dictionaries help our understanding to accomplish a great landing.

Dictionaries are no fool it is a fantastic tool.

Dictionaries enhance the mind, to become brilliant over time.

Motivate one in defining words, intelligent speaking when heard.

Dictionaries gives courage and increases our leverage.

Young, old, blind, will all be remarkable fine.

Information described on every line, no

reason for one to be left behind.

Dictionaries are truly our friend it helps us to grow within.

DID NOT

Did not have my back laid low and relaxed.

Never warmed of trouble the downfall was double.

Changes came my way was nothing I could say.

Did not understand what went wrong and thought I had won.

We were faithful friends, but our friendship turned thin.

Talked a big game, yet it was not the same.

The friendship died long ago, after issues you would not let go.

Did not treat me right, I am going to be all right.

Will get over the hurdles and not be called Myrtle.

Pray happiness continue with you, I will push harder in being true.

DIDN'T GIVE ME A CHANCE

Did not get a chance to be free; they destroyed
our dignity along with me.
Cries of the people were in the air, and it was not fair.
Babies clinging close to mothers, watching
what was happening to others.
Sorrow came on this day did not know why we were hated this way.
Why were we treated so badly? We did not
take anything we never had.
Stood watching families suffering in pain,
tears rolling down faces like rain.
Did not scream or put up a fight because there was no help in sight.
It is just the evil that lies in man, steal one's joy whenever he can.
Did not get a chance that day; our spirits will obtain peace anyway.
Heaven will offer peace, joy, happiness, our
spirits will rejoice everywhere.
We did not get a chance that day but died in Jesus' name.

DISPLEASED

Today dissatisfied, evil took me for a ride, now unsatisfied.

Came in peace, peace decreased, as all Hell increased.

Situations off the chain, nobody with an aim, all playing silly games.

Really wanted to run, to get out of the storm,

before there was serious harm.

Was totally upset, was not a pet, was mad as I could get.

Lost all joy, played for a toy, and the name was not Roy.

Found love was the key, Jesus, and me, only if others could see.

DON'T GIVE INTO DARKNESS

Do not give in often misled, individuals messing with my head.
Do not give in it may not be what you think
and may cause your ship to sink.
Focus on positive things and stay away from dark rings.
Never dwell on discrimination but focus on positive situations.
Run while it is day light, do not let evil take over during midnight.

DON'T CRY

I am getting older as you can see; days are not like they use to be.
I cannot remember as I once did, my knowledge sometimes hide.
Ran hard when there was power, now I am counting every hour.
Mind is on Glory Land, peace, happiness, holding Gods' hand.
May get wrinkle feeble in mind; do not cry because I will be fine.
If I live until old age, it was Christ who set the stage.
When leaving in death do not cry for me, rejoice my soul will be free.
Time for me shall be no more, my soul will
be resting over on the other shore.
Do not cry I shall be at rest because I strived in doing my best.

DON'T UNDERSTAND

I do not understand why one can get it all and others continue to fall.
Do not understand when asking for a dime,
one may have to pay a fine.
I cannot understand how one can leave high school
successful while others leave regretful.
When trying to accomplish goals, all the effort turns crispy cold.
I do not understand when people will put others through
a test, turn and ask them to straighten out the mess.
I do not understand when putting others behind,
saying I am doing you a favor and being kind.
One day will understand, and individuals
will take hold to each other hands.

DO NOT BE AFRAID

Do not be afraid to speck intelligent words,
can be the best anyone has ever heard.
Do not be afraid to use your knowledge and skills,
someone may take advantage and steal.
Do not be afraid to say I am sorry, will not have a reason to worry.
Afraid causes stress, work hard solve the
test, and will dismiss the mess.
Do not be afraid to stand for right, focus with
all might, and never take things lit.
Stand tall do not fall, run the long haul, may be like Paul.

DOWN IN THE DUMPS WITH THE BLUES

As I sat thinking on what went wrong,
blues hit extraordinarily strong.
Information continues to stack as information went slack.
Walked around feeling sorry for self, acting as thou nothing was left.
Could not understand backbiting, criticizing it is
real, and individuals wanting a way to heal.
Brothers misused, knocked down with the
blues, and was nobody fool.
Voice said to hold your peace, wait, Christ will bring a big feast.
Situation will totally heal if following Gods' holy will.
Do not let anyone think it is the end that one will
never win, Christ is going to clean up all sin.
Cannot give up, call it quits think about what one will miss.
Blues can destroy our destination, never let it destroy our limitation.

DREAMS

Imagination thoughts build on wants, to become
successful and controlling the don'ts.
Accomplish a dream, go out with a bang, and the best one ever seen.
May bring happiness on tomorrow, not a future of sorrow.
Dreams create motivation, brings on
communication, a glorious sensation.
Imagine pushing forward, receiving a reward, and joy tickle the heart.
Dreams can be a dream, or fortune and fame, and not a pain.
Dreams obtains serious thinking, without any
blinking, and no time for sinking.
Dream what heaven is like, beautiful city with heavenly
lights, working to see that remarkable site.

ENOUGH

Did a great deed, helping in need, ran into one with greet?
Never thought to look, when you took me
for a loop, stuck me with a hook.
Name was helpful, I became regretful, today, I am thankful.
Rejoiced on thankfulness, never focus on
cranks, and remained with the saints.
Had enough of your stuff, yes trying to be tuff, did not want any fuss.
I know now what to do, do not let deceivers
distract you, and you being the fool.

FAITH

Faith is the substance of things hoped for,
the evidence of things not seen.
Trouble weighs heavily upon the shoulders
and wondering when it will be over.
Our faith put to a test, will not give the heart a rest.
Cannot see the evidence but see protection with-in a fence.
Christ is there when running against the wall,
protect and keep us from falling.
See miracles Jesus perform, must stay
constantly on our heavenly phone.
Keep the faith maintain Christ, will give strength when it rain.
Christ can do all things but fail believe; will have a story to tell.

FANTASTIC DAYS HAS ENDED

Happy days are over, just like a four-leaf clover.
No existing moments anymore, people
constantly walking out the door.
Wars on every hand, individuals stealing, killing, all over the land.
This world is not the same, people are playing silly games.
Prayers going up each day, individuals falling by the way.
This is not a test and people are totally stress.
Christ, gives us chances to get it right, look
around things are getting tight.
Fantastic days has ended, but Christ is going to mend it.
An Angel from heaven will blow the trumpet
horn, finally saints will assemble home.

FEAR

Fear, fear can anyone hear.
Dramatized from fear ringing in my ear.
Fear, fear can anyone hear.
The heart racing with what I am facing.
Will it be over soon or am I totally doomed.
Fear, fear can anyone hear.
Cannot manage the heat, trouble I meet,
will break down into a weep.
Fear, fear can anyone hear.
Will be over soon, wonder for whom, will come with a Zoom.
Fear, fear can anyone hear.

FORGIVENESS NEVER SAID

Forgive me never said, forgive me for being misled.

Blamed others for the wrong, victory was never won.

Misunderstanding always in the way, made it harder for me each day.

Looked in the mirror saw the true you, others saw you as a fool.

Never forget who helped you over the bridge,

protect you from going over the edge.

We will make mistakes, need correction,

must turn into another direction.

We should enhance our fellowman and give them a chance.

FOR REAL

Stormy winds may blow, keep the faith, then mercy will flow.
When Christ comes it is the end, no matter
what you have accomplished my friend.
Christ will be there to pull us through
when things happen like they do.
Everything is for real; individuals say it is no big deal.
Time will bring a body to rest, first make
sure you have done your best.
We are dying one-by-one, closing our eyes to the sitting of the sun.
Even when we do not understand, Christ
is walking with us in the sand.

FURIOUS

Individuals furious in a rage, running around in a daze.
See individuals wrong, and nothing said or done.
No confidence in a friend and become a dead end.
Individuals not seeing their faults never show a second thought.
Problems mentioned, nobody paying attention,
as people moving to another section.
Light bills rent due; nobody is there to help you.
It is impossible to succeed when no help for the needed.
Hatred, stealing has covered the land; good
is now in untrustworthy hands.
Our nation must get serious; individuals are outraged furious.

GRATITUED

Gratitude is thankful; wrong is shameful.

Stealing is wrong; killing is harm.

Dislike is like; climb is hike.

Plant is sowing; grass is mowing.

Dishes means cooking, fishing means hooking.

Dinner is wine, friend's mean kind.

Focus is attention; save is pension.

Demanding work is success; honest destroys mess.

Gratitude produces thankfulness; wisdom produces kindness.

Gratitude means to gain; Bible means sunshine not rain.

GOOD-BYE

Sitting watching as she slowly drifted away, saw hope none that day.

Clinging to one another hoping for a change,

it fell into a different range.

Hearts filled with sadness, eyes filled with tears,

she faded away after many years.

Mother gave joy, happiness along with peace,

yet death continue and did not cease.

We said our last farewell; she closed her eyes, went home with a smile.

GOOD TO BAD

Was intelligent, dependable, now untrustworthy, and unable.

Had money could buy; today I don't even try.

Joy rain down in my soul; now anger took total control.

Never see the righteous forsaken but was a mistake.

Had exciting and wonderful days, then a time bomb came my way.

Spoke well in my time; came a day I spent my last dime.

Wanted to be civil not misused; end up the biggest fool.

Accepted my responsibilities and changed to other activities.

An excellent future planned but other things tore my tree down.

HAD NO IDEAL

No ideal life would be this tough, with struggles in society.

Success placed on the back burner, standing not moving any further.

Lost joy when once obtained, watched hope go down the drain.

Did not realize task would be tight, when working with all might.

Never thought children would relax, never understood worldly tax.

Society issues becoming problems, and no way of solving them.

Not saving a thin dime, while trying to

keep up with the Jones and time.

Had no ideal this would happen, gave in to slack, as issues stacked.

Took peace, joy happiness out, my reaction brought in sadness.

HATRED

Why is there hatred toward me, what did I do to thee.

Saw me as a disease, prayed I did not sneeze.

Did not desire strange looks, watching to see what I took.

Miss understood my capabilities, though I did not have the abilities.

Yes, evil continues toward our brother,

causing war between one another.

We must love from heart-to-heart and push toward the holy mark.

Why not focus on the creator, he is our true maker.

Individuals saw what I was doing, never saw where I was going.

Peace will be one day when Christ gives the okay.

Faith, peace, hope, love will come when entering our heavenly home.

Hatred will go way; darkness will become a brighter day.

HELP IS ON THE WAY

Seek out hope, was no joke, could not grab the rope.
HELP IS ON THE WAY
Life got hard, families spread apart, and pain hit the heart.
HELP IS ON THE WAY
Darkness trouble our society, a wake-up call
for majority, after hitting a variety.
HELP IS ON THE WAY
Situations became tight, people dismissed the
light, and turned toward the night.
HELP IS ON THE WAY
However, individuals looked around, when hearing
that wonderful sound, Christ Jesus is in town.
HELP IS ON THE WAY

HELPING HAND

Helping hands that is me, all that I can truly be.

Give until cannot give anymore, then Christ opening another door.

Bake cakes, pies, delicious meals, food for the bodies to live.

Tired as can be will not stop, yet sometimes

I think I'm going to drop.

Pains attacks this fragile shell must move on and not go to Hell.

Blues will trouble the mind, will run until the end of time.

Total committed working for Christ, will

not become a gambling dice.

HELP ME

I cried "why me" the pain tormented thee.

Called out your name was not ashamed and was not a game.

My heart ached, as I lay awake, wondering
how much more I could take.

Went to God, God help me please; finally, there was a relief.

Down today, up tomorrow, Christ took care of my sorrow.

He took my hand encouraged me to stand;
and I followed his every command.

While help was in sight, did not put up a fight, strived in doing right.

Help changed my attitude and gave me gratitude.

HONEST

Be trustworthy to others as would self; what
you say may damage someone else.
Continue to be honest and fair; will not lose any of your hair.
Never demand with hands on hips, watch what comes from your lips.
Even when individuals speak in hatred, always keep it sacred.
Try to establish a strong bond; one day will sing a new song.
Never take on a matter that may not be
resolved; may go directly to the heart.
It is a time and place for everything no time for ridiculous fling.

HURT

When treated like dirt one will experience hurt.

REMEMBER TO RELY ON THE LORD

Spirit entangled with trouble evil enhances double.

REMEMBER TO RELY ON THE LORD

Going through with pain and see nothing but rain.

REMEMBER TO RELY ON THE LORD

Never let disappointment take over think on a four-leaf-clover.

REMEMBER TO RELY ON THE LORD

Hardships sometimes are strong people think they have won.

REMEMBER TO RELY ON THE LORD

Task is to go through nobody can but you.

REMEMBER TO RELY ON THE LORD

HOW DO YOU SEE ME?

Do you see me tall, short, thin, or muscles fat within?
Do I appear a total mess or in total stress?
Can you see me as a blessing; someone who needs a lesson?
Will be a child who walks down the street
encouraging others as I meet.
Will challenge others to go on, tell them they are never alone.
Will be one to work toward heavenly goals, or wait until I am too old?
Can you see me running a while, not concerned about the miles?
Can you see joy coming my way and will never fade away?

HOW CAN I HELP

Child in the classroom does not care, saying he is not treated fair.
Writing notes, girls talking about boys,
attention should be on books and toys.
How can I help when wanting to put his brother
down, spending monies all over town?
How can I help, when continue to do wrong, talking
about others with that smooth red tongue?
We can help by sharing love, he or she is Gods' angel dove.
We can help in showing affection, and not always giving lectures.
It does not matter if big or small; we could try and help them all.

HELP

You wanted me to die, was not high, and you saw me cry.

Could not speak, started to sink, I became the weakest link.

Name is not Sam, thoughts in leaving town, but went another round.

Nobody really care, choose not to dare, no it is not fair.

Sat and wonder, must I go yonder, wait until thunder?

A mirror of sorrow, cannot even borrow, cannot even hollow.

I need stability, to enhance my liability, and create mobility.

Cannot explain the troubles gained, and really need help in the rain.

Cannot do it alone, need help from the throne, and Christ is the one.

I AM A MAN/MY FATHER'S CHILD

Collaborating with dad was the best days ever.

Saw me as a man working this beautiful land.

Long hard days we put in, it was yesterday and when.

If wrong he corrected me, dad was my hero you see.

Dad is no longer in my life he took an early flight.

Memories I will cherish, and memories will never perish.

Even though it was a short run, I am proud to have been your son.

Help me Lord to live right, so I can rejoice with dad day and night.

You were a father of love; please continue to be my angel dove.

Go on take your rest; loved you, but God loved you best.

Sleep on daddy pain no more; pray that I

will walk into heaven's doors.

IT CAME AROUND AGAIN

Silent and did not say a word, prayed that
my thoughts were not heard.
Lying awake knew it was wrong, thinking on things that I done.
Years went, trouble came my way, thought
about the days father had to pay.
Did not realize how hard it would be, until this matter fell upon me.
Closed my heart to the truth, was busy focusing on the youth.
Thinking that it was over but came back like a clover.
We cannot operate on evil; think we have gotten
by it comes back and ask yourself why.
But for now, do what is right, trouble will not become your nights.

IT CAME

Heartaches came early one morning, clouded and not sunny.

Turned to view what was happening, saw people that was passing.

Death came with a shock it was like losing my favor sock.

It hit did not understand and was truly out of our hands.

Death came as a thief in the night; took a loved one on another flight.

Even thou we lose here on earth, a hurtful lesson we ever had.

Death came soft, sweet, and low, and was no place to go.

We must trust Christ in whom our blessings

flow, be calm and lay low.

Trust God! Trust God! What more can I

say, he is the overseer for all cases.

I CRIED

You saw me cry but did not ask why.
You stood watching, as if you wanted me to die.
Individual cruel with no thoughts of others, went
against the one and only true lover.
Saw me as a used tool, I ended up being the fool.
You were one who knew it all, walked around
as if you were big bad and tall.
Do not think it is all under control, one day
your dreams just may unfold.

IF I COULD GO BACK

If I could go back, would not be slack, will keep emotions on track.

If I could go back would sow more good

seeds, will obtain more deeds.

If I could go back will not dwell on heartaches,

no pain, be pleased with what I gain.

If going back would take away hurt, place it under dirt.

If I could go back, will not stack up junk, would dismiss all the funk.

Could learn to love self-more, from the head to the floor.

Wise in spending monies, not to throw away on hones.

If going back would push to succeed, and constantly read.

After venturing back, found self not going back,

moved on knowing it was the fact.

IMAGINE

Imagine individuals being peaceful and not deceitful.
Imagine not mingling with complainers and not dealing with fainters.
Imagine the world crowded with people of
races, people not moving in a fast pace.
Imagine people stealing, killing, land gaining
attention, not enough food mentioned.
Imagine everything in place, then sorry drops right in your face.
All troubles will fade away, along with bills we now pay.
Can you imagine Christ coming in a little
while; will return in an awesome style.
Imagine those who are right; will see how beautiful heaven is like.

IN THE MORNING

When reality kicks in, no more when, time is over then.
Morning introduced peace, heartaches cease, ends with a feast.
Victory brings joy, saints glorified, not transformed into a toy.
Sun will shine, heaven will be mine, never worry about time.
In the morning will be all right, will catch the
Holy flight, moved into another life.
Every day will be sweet, when saints will be met, with a holy greet.
Conformation is in order, not like any
other, Christ viewing his folder.
In the morning we will rise, and not confused about any size.
In the morning, a bell will ring, white robes I will
see, when the heavenly choir began to sing.

I'M NOT ALL
RESPONSIBLE

Loving you was not hard, until the day you stripped my heart.
Did all that I could do, yet it was not enough for you.
Tried to see if it was me when you wanted to be free.
Worked together for successful things, but
you turned and clipped my wings.
Our love ended, had a flash back of love when, but it was over then.
Our marriage turned to rain, slipped slowly down the drain.
River of tears I cried, knew that I really did try.
Not all responsible when things went wrong
but moved on and became strong.
Was not easy losing my friend yet Christ will be there to the end.

IF ONLY I COULD TALK TO HER

If only I could talk to mother, I would feel better.
Issues I face upon this land, mother would help me to understand.
Mother would say a joyful day is coming and will be as one.
Things is going to be all right, always keep Christ in your eyesight.
Mother would say I saw your tears for years, yes, I am with you dear.
If only I could be there to hold you, however,
God is there when you are blue.
My steps you cannot take, Gods' steps is in his name sake.
My desire is talk to mother, but a conversation
with God will go further.

ISSUES

Why am I going through; issues make me feel blue.

Really try to be strong, yet it is hard to move along.

Stop! Remember what father said, do not worry I am the head.

Disappointments comes in different forms causing serious harm.

This journey will not be smooth, so you must use all your tools.

Never grow tired and give in, never make room for the devil to win.

Issues will sadden the heart, be strong and never depart.

Never think that no one is around, the Lord
is there with a sweet soft sound.

Issues will be faced every day; the Lord will always clear the way.

I REMEMBER

When we were children still at home,
prayed for a moment to be alone.
Washed clothes, cooked, cleaned, using a big bottle of Mr. Clean.
When storms came did not last forever, we took
naps and thought we were in heaven.
We had friends to come and go; we wish we did not see anymore.
Walked to the store in the dark; dreamed of days being in the park.
Looking back as we grew older, realized we had to move farther.
Laughter stole my heart; memories will not depart.
Coming a day of glory land; walking and holding each other's hand.

I SAW YOU

You were sad and not glad.
Showed madness and totally had.
I tried talking to decrease the blues.
The outcome was just like crazy glue.
Expression said, why are you here?
I am not happy when you are near.
I moved on in the Lords' name.
I hoped next time it was not the same.
Christ did intervene; joy came over the scene.
Time was not wasted, when smiles was shown upon the face.

JUST FOR YOU

Do not hate because I am late; look at the time and not the date.

Found out it was your birthday, rushed to make this a special day.

Christ granted this day and made the way

and pray that you will behave.

Kicked heels and made a joyful sound, remember

to thank all friends for coming around.

Hang in there my birthday friend, a true friend to the end.

JUSTICE

Why we are sad, is it because justice we never had?
We were judge and misused, now we are confused.
Nobody grabbed or held our hands, did not
even try to pull us from quicksand.
Jesus is going and will have the last say, no one will speak on that day.
Judgment is coming and why are we sad; look
to the hills rejoice and be glad.

LAST DAYS

Men will believe a lie than the truth, will not get to the root.
Complain about not understanding, never
consider the Lords' demands.
Highway, byway filled with hate; individuals changing mates.
Never give other a chance to survive, never really asks why.
Laughter will slowly fade away, as hatred continue each day.
Society will always ask for more, never realize Christ is the door.
Whatever we do here on earth make sure our rewards are worth it.
Continue to love each, if not, there will be a price to pay.

LAST MINUTE

Saw it coming down the road, just like and old ragged ford.

Wide eyes after me, close as it could be.

No chance of moving out of the way, was nothing I could say.

Glass shattered inside the car; no tools used not even a crowbar.

Blessed as you can see, an angel arms encamped around me.

Christ could have called me home, but time for me had not come.

My friends wear your seat belt in pride,

and Christ will be on your side.

LET IT GO

Let go of disappoints, dismiss ugly comments.
Stop the complaining and start arranging.
Get rid of pit, stop being silly.
No place for sorrow, focus on the tomorrow.
Seek for one who cares, stay away from those unfair.
Never look for hand-outs, always keep God in sight.
Yesterday is truly gone, let us try a different tone.
Be angry sin not, angry will cause one to pop.
Let it go be grateful, grab things that is helpful.
Let it go when individuals do you wrong,
hate will never make you strong.

LIFE MUST GO ON

One may weep, mourn, depressed; will need a little rest.
Disappointments on every hand, wondering where problems will end.
Yells out! Can there be peace? As evil torments the streets.
Society cannot go on this way; please Lord helps us today.
Must go on Christ said so; one day trouble will be no more.
Repentances we will heard if we stay humble and clear.
There will be consolation to know there will be a Revelation.

LOOKED INTO THE MIRROR

Looked into the mirror what did I see, an
angry Black woman tall as a tree.
Could not build body shape to dismiss stress,
did not realize how I got in this mess.
Took another look in the mirror begin to see
hope, turned wrapped away sorrow.
Saw ways of building strong bones, Christ
was not going to leave me alone.
Looked in the mirror saw hope did not see a bar of green soap.
Looked in the mirror saw courage did not
focus on words of discourage.
Looked in the mirror saw a different image, got
a grip and took care of the damage.
Saw an intelligent strong, healthy, encouraged,
straightforward, go getter, peacemaker Black women.
Looked again saw a new beginning, the
Lord and I was truly winning.

MAYBE

Dear Lord, I am at the end, really suffering within.
I need a place to run and hide because I have lost my desires.
I need more of you because you will pull me through.
Need a little conformation to help me to overcome limitation.
Maybe I need to stretch forth my hands so
I can reach the promise land.
Need to get a grip and not hold no one hip.
Maybe I need to gather my thoughts, focus less on wants.
Maybe if I give it to Christ, let him be my
light, then maybe I will be alright.

MEMORIES

Step out of the bed, thoughts in my head, ask Christ to help Fred.

Looking down the hall, waiting for a call, thinking how he stood tall.

Fred Gods' child, carried a serious smile, contact with a dial.

Now it was too late, Friday he met his mate, was his last date.

Oh! Dear brother, was not like any other,

but could not stay any longer.

No more bills he will pay, nothing anyone

can say, will meet again someday.

Sleep on my brother, get your glorious rest,

you lived during your best.

ME

Ran-one complains.

Meditate-one hesitates.

One deceived while others believe.

One yelling while one failing.

One says I need a hand but connected to a destructive band.

Down with destruction with no instruction.

While things are tight others saying it is not right.

A simple situation, but little communication.

All about me and what I cannot do, this is life for all individuals to.

MOTHER'S

Mother's gives instruction manage duration see no limitation.
Mothers are humble and sweet, the best one
will ever meet; will bend to your feet.
Mothers have a graceful heart, will do their part, work, until dark.
Mothers are people who feel pain, comforts
when it rain, and will not go insane.
Real mothers are not like any other, will go a little
further, in storms of dangerous weather.
A mother will keep her child warm, will protect
in harm, and help them to grow strong.
Mothers are wise as can be, strong as a tree, will stand and not flee.
Mothers will guide when wrong, help the child to
move along, joy when the battle is won.
Mothers will get tired, eighteen years of
hired, continue, and not fired.
A mother will take clothes off her back, empty
her sack, so the child will not go slack.
True mothers honor Christ, not like a bowl
of rice, one who paid the price.
True mother is by God, not odd, true love from the heart.

MOTHER'S PRAYER

Mother will not always be there when trouble
falls, so pick up the phone and call.
Mothers pray because we love you, pray that
success will carry you through.
Mothers' prayer will be with you always, until
the end of her promising days.
Asking Christ to watch over her child, please
do not place them in an early file.
Mothers' prayer will travel to the grave, so in your life please behave.
I pray that my child will be strong and will not go but so wrong.

MY CHILD

How can I help when trouble comes your way?
How can I help to brighten up your day?
Will love you with all my heart and will not be left in the dark.
Never claim you to be the best; other pearls are among the rest.
Want my child to be intelligent and become a great legend.
Christ will always give an invitation, even
when facing demanding situations.

MY HAPPY FRIEND

Heart heavy needs a healing, really could not express my feelings.
Met this friend at Central end, now it is a back when.
She greeted everyone who entered the doors,
talked until never no more.
She made you wonder, thoughts of yonder, and things longer.
Packed chicken wings, the largest ever seen tender and lean.
She is no longer on this mountain, never again
will drink from this school fountain.
My friend smiled as she walked out the door, no
kids and attitude will be face with anymore.
A free bird will sing a new song not worrying about what went wrong.
For now, my friend, enjoy your flight, I will be on somewhere in life.

MY HOMETOWN

West Virginia we sometimes go, a state never no more.
Large trees big, green, and wide, roots growing out on both sides.
Mountains huge and completely hulled, traveled
with exciting moments, and never dull.
Going to see family once a year, riding, praying,
and hoping that family did not see fear.
People ask "how can one live here with hills, valleys, everywhere?
Grew up in this beautiful small town, and
our families are not coming down.
You, city folks may think we are crazy,
living in a city that is always hazy.
Working in the mines, not wasting any time we
cannot joke and destroy one thin dime.
For now, West Virginia is still our stumping
ground, we will surely be hanging around.

MY LOVER

Your love is sweet, I am in for a treat.
Your touch makes me whole, causes joy to unfold.
You said I was your Beauty Queen, locked into your dream.
Sweet words you say that really makes my day.
Never wanted for anything, you are my everything.
Your manly voice makes me smile, even after experiencing miles.
How beautiful you are to me, when watching my tall handsome tree.
God sent you my way, was a blessed and positive day.
Will grow together as white feathers, our love hard as shoe leather.
Trouble will appear on our doorstep, yet
Christ will be there to help thee.
Our love will be strong, until Christ say it is time to come home.

MY LOVE

My love, my hero, and joy of today, you
are Gods' servant in every way.
You are concerned when I am sad, say loving things to make me glad.
Worry is not a thing for me, the right words always come from thee.
Sitting and thinking how blessed I am, as
we live peacefully in this town.
Your touch, eyes, and kindness make me smile,
make me want to go an extra mile.
How exciting you make me feel, my love, my friend,
my hero; how can a girl like me give you a zero.

MY PRAYER/
MY MOMMY

I am tiny as can be, your focus is always on me.
It is just you and me, with Christ is makes three.
Pray that God will keep you strong be there
to correct when I am wrong.
We are a team when trouble comes our way,
and prayer always brightens our day.
After reaching old age, will be there to help,
when going through every stage.
Mommy when life shall end, be no more
when, will have lost my best friend.

NEED A RELIEF

Kids struggling to pass tests, tired bodies in this mess.

Wondering why test should be, why can we just be free.

Study hard during the year, test time comes go into fear.

No relief! No relief! The children say, hope

to achieve our goals one day.

Nerves on edge pain in their heads, trying not to be misled.

Twisting, turning, biting nails, feeling faint and turning pale.

Choosing the correct answer is hard, brain turned totally to lard.

Cannot give up, must push on, because we must exit this time, Zone.

NEGATIVE-TO-POSITIVE

Negative people will produce damnation.

Positive people produce conformation.

Negative people will talk down.

Positive people will talk sound.

Negative people will walk in the rain.

Positive people accept the pain.

Negative people choose wrong.

Positive people direction is strong.

Negative people will discourage.

Positive people will encourage.

Negative people will dwell on downfalls.

Positive will dwell on the long haul.

Negative people continue in sin.

Positive people will strive to win.

Negative people take sin as a friend.

Positive people welcome Christ to the end.

NEVER FORGET

Never forget the bridge you came over, the times there was a lover.
Do not forget father and mother mileages,
striving to keep you in college.
Do not always be the one to receive; help others to achieve.
Doors open and one gain; please do not cause others pain.
Never strive on causing harm, never let anyone twist your arm.
Never boast on your success, it was Christ who blessed.
After all accomplishments and success, can
you eliminate backbiting and stress?
The same blessing that came today; never
forget, can be a curse another way.

NO EXCITMENTS

Awake to a beautiful day, knew blessings were coming my way.
Went to work feeling find, individuals were totally kind.
Walked in with fantastic ideals, ladies walking around in heels.
Knew what was on the agenda today, ended up being the sender.
Two-thousand twenty-one excitements decreased,
was like wearing a dog leash.
Go here go there, placed everywhere, no it was not fair.
Joy, hope, laughter, faded away, people having nothing to say.
No more desires to work together, everybody hearts is like leather.
Today excitements are over, individuals trying to stay sober.

NO FORGIVENESS

Prayed for forgiveness, but nobody was listening.
Never express fairness with no ounce of kindness.
Never experience happiness, never express gladness.
Wanted to be right, instead took me for a hike.
Used others knowledge, decreased their
mileage and really had courage.
No forgiveness in this world, thought you was a golden pearl.
Misused and abused many, no escape no not funny.
Will not blame others for things suffered,
Christ the Judge will manage it.

NO TIME

No time! No time! I say, tomorrow will be a brighter day.

No time! No time! To sit and talk, no time for a lovely walk.

No time for getting together, always I will see you later.

No time for things that matter no time for smiles and laughter.

Left in the dark all alone, no one to call on the telephone.

No time! No time! I now see, will anyone be there for me?

Wild thoughts going in all directions, I really love to have affection.

No time! No time! Not for thee, see me as a dead oak tree.

However, one day there will be time, and that day will be all minds.

ONLY CHRIST CAN

Took a heart, started the beat, and now can breathe.

CHRIST CAN

Took the mind, turned it to brilliant, and it made millions.

CHRIST CAN

Took the ocean, put into slow motion.

CHRIST CAN

Took a microscope, looked for dope and planted seeds of hope.

CHRIST CAN

Changed from never, to living forever, place called heaven.

CHRIST CAN

Made sun to shine bright, create mountains

of height, did it with all might.

CHRIST CAN

PATIENCE

Patience is to be still, pray, and chill.

May not see hope today, can be happy anyway.

Do I stop and give up when everything gets tuff?

Never give up the towel, may need it in the next hour.

Patience will run thin but keep Christ within.

Oh Lord! Trying to function but feels like I am in a suction.

Trouble blocks my sight, and the downfalls are not right.

Waiting for a positive side, disappointments cause me to hide.

Heard voices saying go on just dial your telephone.

Patience is what I must obtain, to go through clouds of rain.

Never let it get the best of thee, happiness will appear you see.

No worries of what did not happen, concerns
should be on what is slacking.

Keep faith, patience, and hope, OH! Christ is no joke.

PEACE

Will there be peace, will backbiting ever cease?
Will forgiveness be in this land, causing
individuals to rejoice with holy hands?
Will faith grow stronger, or individuals walking in wonder.
Are we dismissing our blessing, and not learning a serious lesson?
What happen in knowing God, sin has taken us to the dark.
One day if not too late, the heart, soul, and mind will awake.
Seek peace even in the night, Christ will always be the light.
Peace, peace there will be peace, and will be a mighty feast.

PERFECT

Perfect is complete, obtained with no delete.
Perfect can be outstanding, no dips in landing.
Perfect is being right, thanking God for the flight.
Perfect is being wise and will go many miles.
Perfect is standing tall, watching for any falls.
Christ says to try me, see what happens to thee.
Perfect is a way out, through-out your entire life.

PLEASE

Can you help when knowing the fact, please
do not turn and walk back.
No help in seeing me through, when doing all I could do.
Hatred you held inside, and you wanted me to be your guide.
Held me with a fine, treated me as if I committed the crime.
Saw me as a three eyed demon and treated me as not human.
Continue to love when treaty wrong, so I had to remain strong.
Can you stop mistreating me, putting me down,
telling mean things all over town?
Can do worse all by myself; even when nothing is left.
Please help me to understand, however, will survive in this land?

PREDICTION

Predict there will be any more harm, when people learn to love.

Encourage individuals to grab life and hold it with all might.

Stop madness from being the guide; do not commit evil and hide.

Stop using others to maintain wealth and people go into bad health.

Predict peace for the saints, will not be for the cranks.

Stop wiping our brother's faces on the floor,

Christ will come and close that door.

This problem our master will manage, unbelieves will be at his hand.

Society will decrease when sin and the world ends.

QUALIFIED

Am I qualified to teach, or qualified to preach?

Can I run the marathon race, or put out because of slow pace?

Qualified to speak my peace when someone is holding a feast?

Qualified to be the head, or a person who is name Ted?

Am I qualified to think, or would be the one to faint?

Am I qualified to help, while others thinking of self?

Will be qualified because I could, or that I knew I would.

Even when you see me as nothing, I am qualified for something.

QUESTION

You think I do not have a heart, but perfect crumbling it apart.

Saw me as someone you never knew and could not even trust.

What happen to the love that was there, or did it vanish in thin air?

Hate came on board like Never-land, gave up on the helping hand.

Hate! Hate! Became a date and did not come a day late.

Could not understand why this day came, knew

that you did not love me the same.

Trouble increased down the line, and no hope of doing fine.

Oh My! What will become of us when our love turned to dust?

When our love is final will move into another panel.

QUICKLY

Run quickly you are losing time emptiness is close behind.

Emptiness will torment your life, after escaping once or twice.

Heart will continually race swiftly because

emptiness is following quickly.

Go to the left it grabs your hand; tackle you down like quicksand.

Emptiness will not get the best of me, cause

me to dry up like an old tree.

Body will say I quit but will fight on with boxing licks.

Finally rid of emptiness who was behind,

too fast because I never lost time.

REALITY

Hair lay to the side; it was a wedding with a bride.

Dress flowing to the floor; moving as she walked through the door.

Bridesmaid's all shapes, sizes, and color, one for each fellow.

Bridesmaids walked no complaints; make-up glowing upon the saints.

Groomsman dressed to the max as they line up in a stack.

Tall, short, small, or fat, they had it going on like that.

Year's passed wedding over; time to take off the cover.

Together for years and saw tears; stopped calling each other dear.

Will live, love while we can; walk together holding each other hand.

We will be faithful husband and wife until the final stage of life.

These are the facts for today; Christ made it that way.

REGRET

Dissatisfaction one experience, when one did not take me seriously.

Was a BIG mistake when we went out on a

date and found out you were fake.

Thought you were my soul mate, but my feelings ended in hate.

Your attitude took me to the shelf when you assumed I was deaf.

Life for me turned to stone, prayed one day you would be gone.

Viewed the situation between us, found out it was only lust.

A price paid and really regret and the decision I made became a mess.

Open my heart, eyes, and mind thought what I saw was fine.

Oh! Can move away from regret, will think

long and hard before I select.

Went to God in pray, came straight from the

heart, and will not go unsolved.

Talked with God did not go wrong, was thankful overall.

Again, moved from regret, think hard and long before you select.

REMEMBERING

Once there was love, a beautiful white Dove.

Peace glowing over here, happiness flowing over there.

A great summary while working together and did it in harmony.

Kids walking halls in power, glowing like a beautiful flower.

Strived to do their best, never focus on anything less.

Individuals with intelligent smiles, saw smiles coming a mile.

When one cried all cried, tears we did not hide.

Voices of memories in my ear, sweet sounds I loved to hear.

Heartfelt prayers prayed, kept kids from going into a rage.

Looked forward to exiting days, tasks planned in every way.

Wonderful time that never end, with gathering of my friends.

Dressed to impress, red, white, blue lace hanging from the best.

Big holidays, cakes, pies, and chicken and was finger licking.

No one concerned about home, we were off in a time Zone.

Time came memories wiped away; it is now a brand-new day.

Laughter, families, died long ago, and will not be any more.

Love on the back burner, no more striving yonder.

Correction now destroyed; serious matters miss-place.

SEEK ME

Seek me I am waiting, please stop delaying.

Will be your guide, will not run or hide, will walk right by your side.

Saw your tears, felted your fears, never, closed my ears.

Seek me I am your father, will be your mother,

When individuals do you wrong, will give peace

in the storms, will be there in harm.

I am that I am, my name is not Sam, Christ, is who I am.

Stand tall, will not let you fall, will take you through it all.

Seek me seek me, I can help, even when there is nothing left.

Trust in my name, what more can you

gain, life will never be the same.

Seek me seek me, I do have the power, will be there

on every hour, even upon the highest tower.

Seek me seek me, do not be late, I am coming on an

unknown date, gather saints and enter the gate.

SISTER'S

Brought up to be strong, problems we often won.
We had unique needs, taught each other how to read.
Came together when there was sadness,
show affection, love and gladness.
Correct when one was wrong, came together with a song.
Our feet were not of lead, but we all walked straight ahead.
One or two never attended college, but Christ
gave us all profound knowledge.
Developed understanding, demanding
situations and had a great landing.
Sister's a joy to one another, with Christ and no other.

SORROW

Open my heart you closed the door, could not take it anymore.
You took my heart twist it tight; knew it was my last flight.
My love why did it happen this way; picture
walking the isles and marry one day.
I knew without a doubt that you were mine;
you told me we were doing fine.
My heart filled with joy day by day; but trouble came our way.
Saw me as the worse that ever lived; thought
our problems would someday heal.
Sorrow came when you said no more and
watched you walk out the door.
One day you may try to come back, but I will have emptied the sack.
My love, my love what happened to us, was it
being without Christ caused the fuss?

STOOD/NEVER NOTICED

Cried out but did not get the attention.
Did not call my name and never mentioned.
Desires of the heart knocked around and my
abilities stumped in the ground.
Never congratulations for an excellent job;
looked over me and turned to Bob.
Strived in doing my best, intelligence put to a test.
Will not get discourage, will not go off in a rage.
Will remain intelligent and behave, will act intelligent and save.
Went through did not wonder, push hard and grew stronger.
Giving an assignment, stood tall, and may not get recognition at all.
Discouraged will not be always, look ahead and watch for the call.
Never give up stay on this flight; weeping may endure for a night.

SUGAR DADDY

WE children were happy, saving candy wrappers for big daddy.
Dreamed how large it was going to be, splitting
daddy into ones, twos, and threes.
Watched and waited for the post-man to
run, while waiting it was no fun.
Post-man pulled into the driveway; joy filled our home that day.
We kids decided to hang daddy on the wall,
prayed that daddy did not fall.
In school thinking about this large candy,
thinking it was going to be dandy.
Returned home to a loud sound; raced to see what we found.
Daddy fell because of heat; unwrapped and began to eat.
Eating started to complain; teeth were driving us insane.
Went to the dentist got it checked; doctor found holes large as a sack.
Returned home shared daddy upon neighborhood;
mother said I thought you would.
We children still had a smile, even if teeth were in the missing file.

SURE

Sure, enough it came, everyone is drain, individual living in pain.
Sure, enough people lost jobs, Jane, Sue,
and Bob, and took it to the heart.
Sure, enough doors closed, organizations
folded, people pocket full of holes.
Sure, enough people saw it coming, people walked around
harmonizing, others lying on beaches sunning.
Sure, enough people died, others lied, then turned to hide.
Sure, enough individuals became relaxed, everything
spiked to the maxes it is the known fact.
Is there a solution, when people moving in slow
motion, trying to find a solution?
Christ is the solving power, he is dependable, and there every hour.
Sure, enough we need Christ in our lives, someone
who will go every mile, and end up with a smile.
However, continue to pray, STOP! Our sinful
ways, Christ will have the last say.

SIX

Sermon preached; invitation given if right will go to heaven.

Six strong men, with great ambition; walked with a holy mission.

Tall laid back, straight to the max, walked in a marching stack.

Six dressed down in dark uniforms, marched

slowly to a holy song, and was not long.

People ordered to stand like mops, two marched and closed the top.

Six walked out, saw lots of sad faces marched in slow pace.

If you do not have a clue, six will carry a shell, the name could be sue.

In our days we should do our best because

six will escort our shell to rest.

TIME

How long on Lord is it going to be when all my trials will be set free?

Days seem long and dark, everything I do goes to the heart.

Christ is coming on his time, no one will be in the blind.

Prayer will change things because I am under his wing.

Christ is coming in his way, tomorrow or another day.

If only we watch and bear, Christ will dismiss the fear.

Days are like paying a fine, stop the fuss and be kind.

I know you have not forgotten me my soul wants to be free.

Time brings a new song, after we journey home.

Stay calm complete the run, be patience however long.

God will never walk away, so take care until that date.

Until that day, Lord will take his time, and will be worth the wait.

THE CASKET

Walked into the door, eyes looked across the floor;
saw a basket, in the shape of a casket.
Length wide not put together wrong, was for all and not some.
Casket silver, white, gold, black, one for all, line in a stack.
A funeral began, people shacking hands, others came from far land.
Individuals viewed from miles, stayed for
a while, walked down the aisles.
Men lifted the casket by the handle, walked
in sandals, caring it like a candle.
Placed in the ground, covered with dirt, people
standing, faces covered with hurt.
Casket shined beautifully in brass; years
passed now covered with grass.

THE DARKEST HOUR

Oh! My! Oh! My! The darkest hour cannot gain any power.

SPLASH! SPLASH! The water goes, cannot touch my aching toes.

With no desires of wanting to eat, the heart racing with extra beats.

Darkness can take a toll, when seeing life unfold.

HURRY! HURRY! If you possible can,

take Gods' hand he understands.

THE EYES CHRIST WILL WIPE

Pain and hurt often show, problems are well known.
Sadness of eyes never fell, carries burdens so well.
If by chance one loses sight, darkness will be their night.
Disappointments overtakes joy, grace steps in to keep us loyal.
Christ catches every drop if rain; others do not experience pain.
Wait for direction, wait for encampment of protection.
Turned to the left back to the right, the Lord is your sight.
Comfort for sadness, hope for tomorrow, Christ wipes away sorrow.
Christ sees the worries of eyes, deals with hardships and miles.
Although eyes carry grief, Christ carries true relief.

THE HAND

God can touch clouds cause rain, touch the heart cause pain.
Touch the ground assemble a fire; individuals asking why.
Stretch out his hand send down sorrow, one
think there will not be a tomorrow.
Send down a flood, people going insane,
never realizing it was Gods' hand.
Families all in a rage, causing devastation,
trying to find happiness page by page.
Christ can take evil people lower them to affliction,
bring back with a great conviction.
Create a heaven large enough for me; no sin will be there then.
When he comes to gather his pearls, Christ
hands will wipe away this world.

THE LAST SHALL BE FIRST/THE FIRST SHALL BE LAST

I reached for a glass; told to be last.
Went to sit down; told to stand around.
Too overqualified for the job; turned gave it to Bob.
Told me I was nobody, found out I was somebody.
Walk down the street, strangers I see, drop
heads looked down at their feet.
People evil as can be nothing said in defending me.
It is never about achieving; it is about Christ receiving.
But for now, may be last; all of this is coming to past.
Christ will have the final run, and the battle will be won.

THE LAST MOMENTS

The book is open, eyes focus, no sound, nobody hopping.
No one makes a peak, a voice speaks, nobody takes a leap.
Clergy speaks highly of a good man, name could
be Sam, how he achieved with his hands.
Wonderful life he had, worked diligently
and long, now finished his run.
Pushed forward in right, did not take it light,
health decreased during the night.
Family informed; he was gone home, no more to Roam.
Angels instructed, call his name, was no silly game.
Life was not there anymore, no joy to flow, reading
of the last moment closed the door.

THE MIND

A mind with perception, emotion, memory,
imagination, has no limitation.
Mind focuses on what one says, placed in a
memory bank and used for another day.
Mind sends out signals of kindness, and moments of fineness.
Our minds express what we think, sick we cannot blink.
Image losing our though pattern forever,
the body goes into another lever.
Christ gives power, controls the mind, always on time.
Christ gives the brain power to reason, happiness in any season.
Without the mind we are nothing, with the mind we are something.
If losing the mind, life will be no longer, walk around in a wonder.

THE NEIGHBORHOOD KIDS

OH! What a neighborhood we once had, dealt with tough dad.
Gave instruction things to do, did not move until we were though.
We walked the road to our friend's house
and played with field mouse.
When riding the bus each day, prayed for a store stop along the way.
We had friends that lived in the hood, played
with us whenever they could.
We grew up together love in our hearts, true love did not depart.
Families cared for loved one, correct when things went wrong.
Summer came walked to the store, spread goodies
around until there was not anymore.
When darkness came creatures singing, families
sit on porches thinking how amazing.
Our neighborhood kids of age now, with families living out of town.
Neighborhood families be strong hold tight;
will meet again on another flight.

THE ONION

Onions gives flavor, and a true savior.
Onions can be brown or toasted/or placed in a juice roast.
Onions will cause tears, will continue for years.
Onions is an army by itself, will fight until there is nothing left.
The onion is strong a mighty vegetable, capable, and able.
Onions needs no one to watch his back; onion can oversee the pack.
Without onion society could not survive, could take a serious dive.
No onions for the burger, soup, or lamb, even a slice of ham.
Onions considered a loner but comes with an owner.
Onions found all over this land, will continue to have a main plan.

THE PAIN

Thoughts of pain will surely drive one insane.
Not hearing from a loved one or a death call on the phone.
Mistreated by spouse and ends that wonderful life.
In process of a divorce case, hurt written all over the face.
Your friends putting you down and name all over town.
Life melting away like snow, problems facing with nowhere to go.
Pain hit in every direction and will not miss a section.
Maybe too weak to stand; need Jesus to hold my hand.
Christ is my pain killer; will be the pain healer.

THE PIE

Big, blue, with large brown holes, looked like a giant overside mole.

After smelling the golden-brown pie, it was the pie or die.

Decided to eat a huge slice, reaction was not nice.

Body began to tremble and shake; knew that it was a mistake.

Strange pains sweep through my body; sweat

broke out like a serious hobby.

Heart beating extra beats, travel down to my feet.

Saw strange things flying in the air, long blue wild hairs.

Off to the doctor I went; sat me down gave me a hint.

You ate something and needed a flush; if not, you will turn to mush.

Well doctor do what you can, this will not happen again.

THE SEALS

Thinking about the seven seals, when people said no big deal.

See Christ coming a mile away, signs shown each day.

Each seal show Christs' warning and signs of his coming.

Individuals saying it is about abilities but never see realities.

Seeing wrong as right, turning away from the true light.

Mountains of hope falling like rain, people are living in vain.

The blood, the blood creeped in the sea,

caused damnation instead of peace.

Individuals not believing the truth no correction upon the youth.

Until then Christ is warning every moment,

and people should get on it.

THE SIGN INDIVIDUALS HAULED AWAY

People praying never prayed before, saying Lord cannot take anymore.
Individuals confined, homes going into a
rage, while others in a panic stage.
Shelves clean, little supplies, people concerned about their lives.
The sign! The sign! Can we see the Lord it tired of thee?
Individuals hauled away in tracker beds, no breath and totally dead.
The sign! The sign! Can you see them, Christ
coming back no one knows when?
If humbling self and turn from weak ways,
Christ will grant another chance today.
Do not know what is going to happen
tomorrow, today there is sorrow.

THE TREE

I am the tree of life, is visible to all sight.
Limps powerful and strong, will not harm or do any one wrong.
Each branch tells my life history, continues with my life story.
Branches gives grace, as seeing Gods' face.
Leaves offer love, one day fly away like a dove.
Leaves obtains hope, Christ will never say nope.
This tree holds longsuffering and pain, will
guide you through the rain.
This limp gives salvation, does not obtain damnation.
Strong and powerful tree will heal the nation,
when pulling into the right station.

THINK/DO NOT SPEAK

Be calm, never create harm, sang a song.

Misused, do not be a fool, you just may lose.

People watching you, can you be true, see you as blue.

Want to think on great, sitting by the lake, seeing the holy gate.

One will get better, tender as a feather, will go out with laughter.

Say things that matter, watched for later, do not be a hater.

Think do not speak, you will sink, and look like a mink.

Were mad, do not talk bad, will make you sad.

See what is taught, take time to think, with pleasing thoughts.

See self as Gods' child, be mild, and please do not go wild.

THINKING

Thinking when dad, mom, sister, and brother was
around, now I am the only one in town.
One day will be free, chatting with saints I see.
Free of hardships in the land, will rejoice, shaking hands.
Thinking how heaven will be, with brother, sister and yes me.
A set of wings to fly across the ocean, no seasick or motions.
For now, sweet dreams and thoughts, reminiscing
over things that was taught.
A day will come and not alone, a welcome flight will take me home.
Thinking about the joy it will be, picking leaves from the healing tree.

TOMORROW

Tomorrow holds peace that will not cease.
Tomorrow holds success in making a beautiful dress.
Tomorrow brings pain and tamed.
Happiness shall come tomorrow will not bring sorrow.
Tomorrow is for learning and for those who are yearning.
Tomorrow brings gain will be found in Jesus' name.
Tomorrow holds decrease, and an outburst of increase.
Tomorrow I am stronger in Christ and will accomplish a new life.

TORMENTED

Struggling with serious pain, tears falling like rain.

Trouble upon me, crying out, Lord please help me.

Heart tormented in aggravation, drifted from all communications.

Mind yelled insane and could not stand the horrible pain.

How long can this pain last, will it ever come to past?

Sink deep into sand; could not grab anyone hands.

This mark will linger through my time, established in my prime.

Have no prediction how life will fall and

know that this is not the last call.

TOSS

Sad because of loss; our hearts and minds tossed.
Did not understand what happened like it did,
everything was in order and not hid.
Blamed others for trouble in our lives, bitter when our loved one died.
Time is coming for every man; we need to take hold to Gods' hand.
Not to worry about things on this side, we
are the only one that will ride.
On this side we are tossed, but on the other side none is lost.

THE QUESTION

Can I attend regular school or be a fool?
Choosing friends over school; dismiss precious tools.
Strive in blaming others for wrong, fix it and move on.
Father and mother supplying needs and kids like dead seeds.
Will continue to run with the gang or go into a different lane?
Must I accomplish something or continue to be nothing?
STOP! Get a grip stay in school and do not trip.
Focus on your life not things which will cause one strife.
Work hard moves swiftly along and continue to be strong.

TRAPPED

Trapped, trapped cannot get out!
Can not see or move about and tears are rolling down my face.
Trapped, trapped Lord help me please, I really want a relief.
Please somebody grab my hands, help me to understand.
See nothing but strange land, no one with a solid plan.
Never though it would go this far, never realize it would be this hard.
Trapped, trapped, what must I do? Strike up a
conversation may help me through.
Makes me think I am finish when darkness is saying I am winning.
Trapped, trapped know who can help, he is
in the right and even in the left.
Christ will heal all pains and will walk out of the rain.
Trapped and will escape, our father is never late.

TRUST

Saw you as my friend, prayed with me through thick and thin.
Trusty you in my name, did not worry about a thing.
You gave up precious time, walked me through mine.
Complain, I will not, your friendship carried me though a lot.
Trust is powerful, spiritual, sacred, a word that is heard.
Depended on your ability, relied on your stability.
Believe on day I will unfold, and from there will have control.

TRUE

Was it true when you said you loved me; would
be there in what I went through?
Was it true when you said in sickness or health,
remain with me if there was no wealth?
Was it true if I had doubts in mind, you
would be there to comfort in time.
Was it true even when given bad advice, you would be there for life?
Was it true before dying of old age, would not die with rage?

THE PURPOSE
OF A FAMILY

The purpose is not to see what one can gain; hurt another with pain.

To walk side by side, never say things that one may hide.

Work together with all might; do not say
things that will cause a fight.

Speak to unsaved family about time; something
to ponder deep in their minds.

To push for higher mountains and drink from the Holy fountain.

Family must do right, with all might, will not become one's night.

Especially important to be humble, will not go out in a stumble.

When the family chapter has ended, our chapter's will be over then.

WAITING

Waited for a letter to come; believed that someone else had won.

Heart ached when you left when you focus more on self.

Was a price I had to pay as you walked out that day.

When it became one, two, and three; found

out you wanted to be free.

Was played for a toy, worked to fill our house with joy.

You will not destroy my heart or cause joy to depart.

Waited but waiting is over and not ready for another lover.

However, someday, somebody will be in my

life, love and want me for a wife.

WE CANNOT
CHANGE IT

Cannot change the moon when shinning at
night; it helps to bring brighter light.
Pray that the Lord will step in on time when
a bad thought pops in the mind.
Cannot stop a drunken man when wanting a
drink, day will come when health sinks.
Cannot control a child when married and gone,
may come back with a different tone.
Cannot chance the hairs numbered on our
heads, time comes will rest in our beds.
Cannot change heartache we feel, not and orange we sometimes peel.
Cannot change the way people love, individuals treated like Doves.
After missing his car, a hundred-dollar bill,
an angry man may want to kill.
Cannot change diseases that pull one down,
if dying in Christ will have a crown.

WE WONDER WHY

Individuals are not selected and will be rejected.

Faced with lectures and skipped over in the future.

Wonder why individuals are abused, thinking they are fools.

Children with no abilities to shine; or maintain a clear mind.

Cannot see the needs, too busy planting evil seeds.

People stealing, killing, no plans of healing.

People against one another; love walks out the door.

Why not look forward in loving me, and not seeing a tragedy?

Oh! You got it now; well I will see you around.

WE MAY NOT UNDERSTAND

May not understand what comes our way
and bring sadness on a sunny day.
We must remain strong even when sorrow comes along.
God will be there through every mile, even
when hurt linger for a while.
May not understand the things we go through
and sometimes leave us blue.
Christ will be on time, even when we are at
the end and bring a relief with-in.
Christ is there to ease the pain, even when walking in the rain.
We may not understand how the Lord works;
all we need to do is be alert.

WHAT CAN I DO?

After everything said and done, made my last run.
WHAT CAN I DO
When walked the last hall, no more notes or calls.
WHAT CAN I DO
All laughter decreased; death has increased.
WHAT CAN I DO
Saw clouds fade away; tomorrow became another day.
WHAT CAN I DO
Disappointments I now see; no more peace for me.
WHAT CAN I DO
Asks God for help, he is the only one left.
WHAT CAN I DO
Christ took care of my trouble mind and now doing fine.
WHAT CAN I DO
Situation did not go well but will have something to tell.
WHAT CAN I DO
Trouble lasts for a while but now it is in Gods' file.
GOD DID IT!

WHAT CHRIST EXPECT

When we assemble; Christ expects us to be humble.
Dismissing the whining go out being kind.
Treat our fellowman right, and never ever slight.
Show a friendly face, not a face with a bad taste.
Never look depressed; bad spirits rub off on the best.
Look and see hope, never see a slope.
Christ expects us to have ambition and with determination.
Peace happiness from head to floor, pray that unsaved
individuals will come through the door.
Christ expects us to see others as somebody
and never see others as a nobody.

WHAT IS WRONG

I am confused, totally misused, must overcome subdued.

Joy did not find, attitudes of many kinds, others with loud whines.

Laughter slipped away, brought sadness today, nothing I could say.

Obstacles obtained, life never the same, courage I must gain.

A grip I must get, cannot stop or flip.

Will be stable, focus on being able, never see self as a label.

Wait for the morning sun; find out what went

wrong, then disappointments will be gone.

Walked in the light, took on height and viewed another sight.

Decided not to go back, picked up the slack, carried joy in my sack.

WHAT IF

When I cried out in pain; will you think I am insane?
When trouble within, would you reach out then?
When walking the floor all night, could not focus
on right, will you make my burdens light?
If I could change one's mind, did it in time, would they be fine?
If there was no depression, with no rejection,
would there be any connection?
What if peace was here, laughter over there, and no crime anywhere.
However, if peace is what we need then Jesus must be our seed.

WHAT YOU DO WILL NOT STOP ME

Knock me down will not stop.

Build mountains will get to the top.

Cause hurt, treat me like dirt, not going to be a jerk.

May cause one to feel sad, Christ will make me glad.

Think I am down for the count, must have more than that amount.

Say what you will or may, Christ will make my day.

This attitude will not cause me harm, when you think you have won.

God prepared me for critical days, strengthen me in going all the way.

Cannot let evil words cripple me, encourage me to go extra you see.

What you say will not bring me down, one day

will have new residence in another town.

WHEN DEATH SHALL COME

Wondering how it is going to be when death creeps upon thee.
Body becomes as steel, not one pill will be able to heal.
Shelf will slowly fade its color, give off a strange odor.
Eyes wall back in the head; everyone know I am dead.
Soul moves to eternity and will leave out with dignity.
Imaging weeping all around and people
crying with a soft echo sound.
Do not attempt to look for me, will be in the arms of thee.
Heaven a beautiful place, will see Jesus' face to face.
Will receive a glorious robe that day and bills I will not have to pay.
Will sing glorious songs, nobody will be wrong.
Heavenly choir will greet, meet, holding hands,
and join in the Christian band.

WHERE AM I

Walked off could not remember direction;
no one to guide me to my section.
Intelligent and could think, body in need of something hot to drink.
Was stable yesterday knew where I lived, today
the mind went on a brief chill.
Lived alone in my tiny home, now can not
call a friend on the telephone.
Confused can not find my way; needed
help in getting to safety that day.
While walking took a moment to rest; sat down saying this was a test.
Tried to accumulate heat; so tired, fell into a deep sleep.
Dreamed being in my warm bed; wrapped
under a blanket pulled over my head.
There all doing the night; went on a trip,
now pills I will not have to skip.
Alzheimer diagnosed not to be furious; it is a disease that is serious.

WHY HAVE ENEMIES

Enemies keeps us down on the knees, bending as a rugged tree.
Enemies help one to grow in grace move in a steady pace.
Enemies help one to keep the mouth closed
and watch miracles unfold.
Enemies give us inspiration while going through durations.
Ditches set for saints to fall into, one is prepared for the enemy to.
Christians obtain power from heavenly sources
and control by the universe force.
Now you know why enemies are around we must stay sound.
Our souls will not drown, if not letting our guard down.
Never say we have it made; enemies will wait in the darkness shade.
Be safe and not to be merry; enemies will be in a hurry.

WILL IT COME A DAY?

Will individuals stop looking down on
another, stop brutalizing each other?
Hope that success will come our way; after pushing hard each day.
Will attention be place on the positive side
or more attention on the negative?
Will come a day where people will achieve, not turn out as a deceiver.
Will humiliate, disappointments, dissatisfaction be
place behind, we then can turn with clear mind?

WITH IN

Face of happiness shine today, hurt with-in shine always.
Peace, joy, and affection will come in all
direction and will bring affection.
Small candles shinning all during the night,
knew that I would be all right.
Individuals see me as fine, yet the heart is broken and not kind.
Did all that I could do, knew that you were not true.
Weeping never shown on the face, carried inside with a bitter taste.
Did not show emotions; God will helped me to function.

WHEN TIRED OF BEING TIRED

When tired of being tired, then one can live.
Strive in reaching goals, will not let my purpose fold.
Will pick self-up and not think everything sucks.
Will not let discouraging words pull me down, will go another round.
Will not look at self as doomed cannot allow the room.
Not allow sickness to get to me, and waste away as if an old tree.
I am tired of wallowing in pity, so dust off, try another city.
When being sick and tired Christ will grant power, strength,
courage, understanding, and there every hour.
Will give Christ thanks for all he is doing, until my last running.

WILL HAPPENS TOMORROW

When tomorrow is not for me, pray that I will be with thee.
When no tomorrow comes my way, have transformed that day.
When tomorrow comes, will go home, no more days to Rome.
On tomorrow will be peace, joy, happiness and wipe away all sadness.
When tomorrow comes no more loneliness, will only be safeness.
Tomorrow is coming do not know when,
when it comes, I will be ready then.
Lord preparing us each day, will guide us in his Holy way.
Tomorrow will be marvelous time, when
shaking hands and no crime.
What happens tomorrow will be all right,
cling to Christ he is dynamite.

WILL YOU EVER LOVE ME?

Moved everything to win your love, treated you as my heavenly Dove.

Gave everything a person could give, said I

was one of the worst that lived.

Went as far as washing your clothes, took

time to clean your dirty toes.

I gave my last dime in making you happy, you turned and snapped.

Tried becoming a role model for you, instead you made life blue.

No communication between us, was not civil always a fuss.

Love was not on board, angry words took the higher road.

You never loved me the way I loved you, you were not even true.

We decided to go our separate ways, departed with few words to say.

Found out you really did not love me, oh!

But there will be someone you see.

WHO SAYS WE CANNOT?

Who say we cannot be the one to walk the moon,
the same one to challenge the doom?
Who says we cannot preach to the wealthy,
whose lifestyle sometimes unhealthy?
Who say we cannot be the one to correct, the one to direct?
Who says we cannot build the highest building,
provide poor people a decent living?
Who says we cannot save a life from sin; that soul the Lord will win?
Who says we cannot get a child off the street, that
child will encourage everyone they meet?
Who says we cannot give our brother a hand,
even if it interrupts our plan?
Who says we cannot climb the highest mountain,
and drink from the Holy fountain?
Who says we cannot cherish the old, we will fall into that mold?
Who say we cannot love Jesus if right and with all might?
Do not say what one cannot do; look around it just may come true.

WHY PRAY

Prayer will give us strength, to conquer challenges we meet.
When going through temptation, prayer will be our consolation.
Prayer is speaking to God in adoration and with no limitation.
Prayer is thanking Christ for all he does, asking
for consideration for enemies to.
Prayer is when one is making a request, asking
for grace when going through a test.
Prayer is real powers, will work on every hour.
With prayer one cannot go wrong, it really makes us strong.

WORTHY

Having valuables, and praise, it increases on another raise.
A person with prominent position, others in smaller condition.
Having power to be great, on time and never late.
Worthies create faithfulness, will not create craziness.
Worthies! Worthies! The Lord is great,
food for our souls, all must eat.
Worthies is the Lamb we must say, Christ will make a way.
Worthies always intervenes; Christ the best we ever known.
Love of Christ runs through our veins;
controls the mind and keep one save.
Worthy! Worthy! He is the Lamb, be ready
will be back without a sound.

WONDER WHY

I knew why you left, you wanted to be free and
was nothing in your heart for me.
I know now why we grew apart, everything said turned to lard.
Really wanted to be a loving wife, however,
you were the worse in my life.
Never dreamed this day would come when
our house was no longer a home.
Hard times goes with marriage and do have words of encourage.
Wonder why you could not love me; beautified self just for thee.
Years passed showed no affection moved into another direction.
Did not our love grew weak and knew we were at our lowest peak.
Okay now will move farther and accomplish stormy weather.

YESTERDAY

Yesterday no fear, no backbiting in the air.

Everybody on one accord, did not take issues to the heart.

Yesterday things were okay and looking forward to another day.

Everything smooth and right, everything looked good insight.

Yesterday believed in shame, today running a different game.

Yesterday pushed to obtain, now drop to pain.

Yesterday pushed to maintain, now no hope, nor gain.

Yesterday on point, today do not know what one want.

Yesterday had options and power, today cannot chose a certain hour.

YOU ARE SPECIAL

Christ grant strength, never walk as the weakest link.
Look over by many, Christ blessed with plenty.
I am special in Gods' sight he is my guiding light.
Will love family and friends will be there until the end.
Christ is on my side, truth he does not hide.
Special, Christ said so, when not able to
manage failure, he is at the door.
When Christ gives the final word, it is just what he said.

YOUR CAN'T STOP IT

Wonder why things happen like they do,
trials, tribulations fall upon you.
Give up is not a good thing; get up yell dance or sing.
You cannot stop pain when falling your way;
will demolish your beautiful day.
One asks why it's hard for me when others are being free.
Times are tight bills due; ride out the storm Christ is with you.
Times are not like they use to be hills rocky people stocky.
Stand until your day is done, will know that today I won.

YOU DID IT TO ME

I trusted you, I thought you were fair, never
thought I would pull my hair.
Gave information and followed behind, no
communication along with time.
Push hard to make it work for me, shade
covered my eyes, and could not think.
Blind-sided did not see it coming, could not even turn to run.
Trust was not in your book; information
was gone with no second look.
Mind said quit while you are ahead, heart
said you been totally misled.
Put behind the entire let downs, move on without a frown.
You may have done it to me this time, watch
your back you may be in the next stack.

YOU LEFT ME

Tears streamed down my face in a daze, as
I saw you packing your suitcase.
Our best days you decided to take a flight,
did love you with all might.
Situations we could have faced together,
you looked and said whatever.
Now sitting watching the four walls, imagine
hearing footsteps coming down the hall.
Sadness flowing from every room, asking why it happened so soon.
Pain of hurt filled my heart and will obtain a huge scare.
Never imagined pulling off my rings, found
out you waned other things.
Realize now there will be no more dreams,
when going to order Ice Cream.
You left me hoping to achieve better; now
this will be my final note in letter.

YOU

You were kind, when out to dine, we spend wonderful time.
Showed romance, when out on a dance and was not the last.
Gave wonderful gifts, loving words fell from the
lips and monies came from the hips.
Yes, a beautiful person, will love any season, with no certain reason.
Became my soul mate, it was a date, life moved on great.
Love grew stronger, never wonder, life for us grew longer.
See what Christ can do, he saw us through, now it is me and you.

YOU CAN'T

You cannot lose with the stuff we use, end up confused.
Using your abilities to maintain, with
knowledge, power we shall gain.
Given a pen, create a thought, address it to Lin.
Cannot lose what one gain and go down the drain.
Wisdom, knowledge, understanding create
destination and a smooth landing.
Why lose intelligent thoughts, go out with words of intelligent wants.
This is a lessoning, can be a blessing, if only one will listening.

YOU SHOW ME

Show me where I went wrong, really want to be strong.

Guide me, direct me, then will move along and effort will be won.

Do not fully understand all information;

need more than an illustration.

Please be patient, give me time, will get off milk and will be fine.

Push to do what I can, even when raising my hands.

Can anyone show me what to do, right now feel

like I am locked in an animal Zoo?

You will help me to improve self; this is the only option left.

Show me how to accomplish my task, then

will no longer need a mask.

ZIG ZAG

Was your character, saw me as laughter, there here after.
Went from being straight, chose other dates, now it is too late.
Wish to be correct, had desires of not being
sad, but thoughts of being mad.
Saw me as a pad, I was your child, and been had.
Just like a puzzle, splashing though a puddle,
with outstanding struggles.
Went from being encouraged to discourage and never found leverage.
I regained strength; power rebuild now I am not a ZIG ZAG link.

Fin

MY RESUME

My name is Christa L. Tarpley, and I was born and raised in the state of Virginia. Four-years of college (National Business college and Phoenix). A mother of two daughters, my dream has always been to write things that will encourage others to see hope (even if they think there isn't any) and know that joy will always come in the morning. I believe writing is a passion to express feelings, and can testify that a song, play, poem, or even a children's book can be uplifting during hard times. I enjoy what I do and hope to keep doing what I love for as long as I can.

Thank you for reading!
C.L. Tarpley

www.ingramcontent.com/pod-product-compliance
Lightning Source LLC
Chambersburg PA
CBHW021636120626
46545CB00002B/577